STAND AT EASE

RAJNEESH JASWAL

Made with ♥ on the Notion Press Platform
www.notionpress.com

Dedicated to dear friend Amit Nag, whom we lost many a time before we finally lost him in a deadly bike accident.

Contents

Acknowledgements

Thanks to Kavya Rajneesh Jaswal (my daughter) for designing the cover. Thanks to my wife Ranjana, and daughter Shravya for extending all help.

Prologue

5.30, early in the morning; the playground just above the river Beas would send shivers even in the month of September, much before the official arrival of winters. Half sleeve T-Shirts and white shorts below-belt, the mandatory attire for morning drills wouldn't simply do enough to counter the biting cold.

It was only a couple of rounds of the ground that day for the warm-up. Rest of the drill was called off, for there were some important instructions to be given particularly to the newly joined batch of class 6.

'Attention!'.....(a long silence prevailed with that command from the front),

'Look straight.'(Silence deepens further).

'Chest out!.....'

"You mustn't see the neck of person standing third next to you. This is your first day on the ground and instructions won't be repeated," thus commanded the Physical Education teacher.

Mr. Sandhu, our physical education teacher (PET) he was. A cut surd Punjabi, Mr. Sandhu was tough and stout as they generally are. Mr. Sandhu, a young bachelor was a fitness freak himself. He would follow the ground routines religiously. Tall man, his body in shape, clean shaven with trimmed moustache, Mr. Sandhu had his cheek bones out. His haircut had allowed his otherwise curly black hair to look pointed. His track suits used to be nicely laundered and ironed; fitting to reveal his perfectly toned body shape. Mr. Sandhu would speak a mix of Hindi and English wrapped in Typical Punjabi accent.

For the newly joined class six, this first morning drill was more like an unpleasant surprise. The little boarders who were separated from their parents at this tender age, were supposed to spend seven years in this Coveted residential school called Navodaya Vidyalaya.

Though not to mention, they were here after having cleared an entrance exam. The result however, despite being good didn't actually taste good. They were yet to come to terms with their parting away from their parents, siblings, friends, and from their beloved homes. Mr. Sandhu hadn't allowed them the time to adapt to the situation and had started calling his shots from day one, straightway, introducing them to the regimented life which was in the offing, much like that of a cloister.

"Class six will stay and rest all may start their rounds", Mr. Sandhu with that order made us to stand in three queues (popularly called in-threes), height wise, separate for boys and girls.

"Attention!" his robust and husky command would naturally mean a jerk that would straighten the back, stiffen the thighs, would lift the neck a few degrees, and hands clenching into fists.

"This is the standard trouping you are supposed to move in, from hostels to ground, from ground to hostels, from classrooms to mess, from mess to classroom, from classroom to morning assembly or from morning assembly to classroom. Whatever be the destination, inside the campus you will move 'in-threes' only." The message was loud and clear from Mr. Sandhu.

"*Stanteas!*", commanded Mr. Sandhu but no one of us moved as no one of us could get what he meant by that command.

I was fairly tall but not the tallest. The last man in my row whispered in my ears without actually moving an inch, "What did he say?" I didn't dare reply, fearing Mr. Sandhu might take notice of it, and moreover, even I didn't understand what he actually meant by the command- 'stantease'.

Sensing the lull, Mr. Sandhu quickly deciphered it for us, "move your feet apart, put your hand behind your back and feel relaxed."

"Oh! He meant *Vishh-raam*", man behind me again whispered, to actually irritate me this occasion. I wanted to see him, who was the man who dared to speak a few things in such prohibitory conditions, but turning my neck 180 degrees would have been an offence. He was the only man to do that from a batch of eighty odd students.

How the life would be in Navodaya was almost decoded early in the morning on day one, including the word *stantease*, before we marched past into our hostels, baffled and stupefied.

CHAPTER ONE

THE LAST MAN TURNED FIRST

The moment we reached our hostel I took notice of the man I wanted to. He was tall, dark, and tough built man who obviously looked older for the age group supposed to be in class six. Some traces of whiskers could be noticed on his pointed face. Though slim, he wasn't skinny. His shoulders were broad but he would walk slightly bent. His hairstyle was duly taken care of, with a puff falling on his forehead. He actually saw me taking note of him and we exchanged smiles; still we didn't talk to each other.

It was in the classroom actually where I discovered that I would be sharing desk with the man himself. We were a new class altogether and therefore there were lot of introductory rounds. It was revealed in the process that he was Amit Nag. He hailed from Gumma, a place famous for salt mines in district Mandi of Himachal Pradesh. He seemed fairly acquainted with all the specialties of his place and was extremely vocal narrating them whenever he was asked to introduce himself. His surname, Nag sounded unusual to some, so it also at times made a laughing stock of him amongst few quarters. He however loved it and it only made him to tell more and more about him.

In one of the classes when we were made to perform some activities, Nag surprised everyone with his dancing skills. "Break Dance", as he would call it, made everyone laugh. Teachers were already appreciating him and Nag was certainly enjoying this. He revealed that he had learnt his dancing skills from Michael Jackson, whom he followed on television.

To Nag's introduction, there was a dark side as well. He had lost both his parents and was being brought up by his married elder sister and brother in law. This also generated a kind of sympathy for him but that again added to his fanfare.

It was during the break that I got an opportunity to talk to Nag.

"Why do you suffix the surname Nag to your first name? I haven't heard of this before." I quizzed.

"We are the worshippers of Nagas-the serpents, supposed to be the descendants of Vasu and Takshaka. In Hindu mythology there are eight Nagas (serpents) -Shesh, Takshaka, Vasuki, Vajra, Danshana, KarKotik, Kemmali, Sankhu and Kali. The places inhabited by us are called *Nagnis*. We are pundits actually but we are different on many accounts from other pundits. For example we are non-vegetarians unlike other Brahmins. We also don't mind consuming alcohol in marriage parties or other ritualistic gatherings." Nag explained so vividly that I was left awe-struck.

I didn't know anything about my origin. I didn't even have my surname suffixed to my first name in official records. Nag was all proud to trace the origin of his descendants, while simultaneously bragging that he was a highborn.

It was the next morning when Mr. Sandhu took a preliminary Physical endurance test of us. We were made to run, to skip, to jump, to throw, to wrestle and so on. To my surprise Nag stood atop. He could run quickly, skip fast, jump long and high, throw accurate and a fair distance, and could wrestle to ground his opponent. Mr. Sandhu's smile confirmed that Nag was his pick amongst the new group, the prodigy he was going to train for next inter school sports meet.

Mr. Sandhu's group or the 'sports group' was an elite group, which used to enjoy many privileges. They would follow a diet slightly different from others. An extra milk packet and an egg a day would envy rest others. They could play even during the morning drills while all others had to sweat doing running and aerobics. Besides, they were treated liberally by other teachers, while submitting their assignments and home works.

Nag was straightway chosen the sports captain of our class. He was to command us whenever our troupe would march past every single destination in the periphery of the campus.

While many of us were still lamenting the separation from our beloved ones, Nag had emerged as a leader. He was also tasked with the responsibility of taking care of those who were finding it difficult to adjust to the conditions. He was also giving us tips on athleticism and other sporting activities. He was also being invited by seniors for performance, especially his typical Break dance. Many senior girls were looking for opportunities to talk to him. Nag had in no time become the popular most face of the school.

CHAPTER TWO

Nagroom & the Visual Display Unit

Nag was already calling his shots. There was no one who could defeat him in 100 meters race even up to class VIII. The only two from the entire school were from class IX, which was the senior most class as Navodayas were established three years back only. The proximity with other sports persons introduced Nag to his seniors and at the same time to their misdoings as well. Hiring VCR on rent and watching movies was one such thing which was highly popular amongst students.

Nag on the pretext of studying would walk into the hostels of seniors and end up watching movies, the latest Bollywood hits of nineties. We did have a recreation room but we were allowed only one movie a week and that was only on Sundays. Nag would score over rest of us and would narrate stories of the movies we missed out on.

Sometimes even sharing of comic books also formed part of hangouts available to us. Nag had access to all new releases of Nagraj, Super Commando Dhruv, Chacha Choudhary and Sabu, Lambu-Motu series and many others, and would circulate them inside our hostel.

We were housed in Raman House, in four different yet very close type-III residential buildings which for the purpose of identification were earmarked as P-1, P-2, P-3, and P-4. The regular premises for the school were yet to be constructed by CPWD (Central Public Works department). We were therefore housed in make shift buildings of BBMB (Bhakra Beas Management Board).

Just in the vicinity was a Dam called Pandoh Dam, which was part of Beas-Sutlej link project. An underground tunnel from the Pandoh Dam opens up as a canal on the other side of a gigantic mountain passing through entire Balh valley of Mandi District, to facilitate the irrigation of the adjoining areas. It joins Sutlej at a place called Slappar where it generates electricity also. The dam was constructed in the year 1977 and it was due to this that a colony called BBMB colony was constructed for the officials.

Navodaya Vidyalaya Pandoh was housed in some of the dilapidated buildings of BBMB. These buildings were actually abandoned by the Board and were therefore hired by Navodaya Vidyalaya Samiti. After some minor repairs and restorations these buildings were allowed to serve the entire premises for the school. Land acquisition was still in the process of completion and that's why the award for works of new constructions was getting delayed.

We were in P-2, a type three building, having three bed rooms, a dining hall, one very small store room, a kitchen which was turned into bathroom, a dedicated bathroom with attached toilet, and one more separate toilet outside. Each bed room was fitted in with four double decker beds. Therefore each bed room was housing eight students. The room originally meant for dining, was fitted in with two double decker beds housing four students. The very small store room was also fitted in with a single double decker bed housing two, including our sports prefect, Amit Nag. So all in all we were 30 odd students who were housed in P-2.

Nag's sleeping chamber, or the Nagroom, was well inside one of the bed rooms. Therefore the route was the main gate, the dining hall, the bedroom, and then into the Nagroom. Obviously Nag had to cross two rooms whenever he entered after those late night outs at senior's hostel especially on Saturdays, and that made many of us aware about his adventures. Nag tried to be as safe as he could but still it wasn't wise with many small kids around who would report everything to warden, especially with those typical toppers every class has.

However, the small store room inside had many advantages as well. It was not easy to check or carry out the search operations which were quite popular among some wardens. Nag would keep his trunk box full of comic books, just above his bed on a cemented rack which wasn't even visible at times. Still anyone entering on a tip off or with the intent of random checking would find it hard to take a look in Nag's trunk box as it could only be sighted after climbing on Nag's bed which of course was the upper berth of a double decker bed.

Nag had many a time discussed with me the probability of getting in without being noticed but perhaps there wasn't any way. Getting in from behind was not a possibility as Nagroom had no window.

Sawan Singh Mand was the warden in-charge from P-1to P-4. P-1 and P-2 were inhabited by class VI, while P-3 & P-4 by class VII. The boys of class 6 and 7 were looked after by Mr. S.S. Mand, that precisely meant.

Mr. S. S Mand was a Sardarji who was into his second service after retiring from army. Although he was from the non-teaching staff, yet he was made warden by the Principal. He was actually a pharmacist who took care of primary health needs of students. Mr. Mand didn't enjoy a good equation with Mr. Sandhu and this was the obvious reason for his hatred towards sports persons.

They would both pick up a quarrel over small petty issues. It once assumed serious proportions as Mr. Mand landed a powerful punch on Mr. Sandhu's face in the common mess hall after a brief altercation. It left his lower lip bleeding. Mr. Sandhu wanted to retaliate but some of mess cooks intervened to take him away. He had waited the entire day standing outside for Mr. Mand but he never came as he was stealthily taken away by other teachers.

Mr. Mand was not as athletic as Mr. Sandhu was, but like Mr. Sandhu he also was extremely gutsy. It was a difficult choice who would emerge victorious, in case the scuffle turned physical. Some of the students were desperately waiting for this clash of titans.

Mr. S.S Mand, though he wasn't into the routine soldiering, was still a trained army personnel. However, his age wasn't on his side and worst, he had put on some extra weight. He was average high with good health like all Punjabi's, but wasn't as agile as Mr. Sandhu was. He still had proved his worth by taking the lead, as he was the one who attacked first and had landed a punch on Mr. Sandhu's face.

Mr. Sandhu wouldn't forgive easily, vengeance was in his mind and he always looked for opportunities. Other day, on just a minor altercation Mr. Sandhu had jumped shoulder high to land a flying kick on Mr. Mand's chest but it didn't connect as his attack was foiled by the intervention of other teachers and both were immediately taken away.

The exact reason for their rivalry was not known but some of the seniors would claim that it was the ma'am beautiful (one lady teacher so named by students), who was the bone of contention. Ma'am beautiful would pass her hypnotizing smile to both the sirs in a non-partisan manner. She most possibly had a fair idea that it was she being contested.Their ego however clashed on different issues and ma'am beautiful wasn't the only dispute. Rift was enlarged, so much so that Mr. Mand won't appreciate students of his hostel joining sports.

"Life is all about studies; you will get plenty of opportunities to play, but little to study if you miss this time." This was how he preached one fine evening after the evening prayers. The evening prayers were a ritual which was followed by complete blackout after which students had to mandatorily sleep.

This conflict of interests had put Nag in Mr. Mand's bad books. He was looking for opportunities to nab him. Once he got one, he would take Nag to Principal and would plea that he was detracted because of sports, shifting the entire blame on Mr. Sandhu.

Other peculiar thing about Mr. Mand was that he would punish everyone for anyone's mistake. Entire seven and six class could be seen frequently hanging upside down against a wall, sometimes doing front rolls, sit ups, or mostly squatting, looping their arms behind their knees holding their earlobes (Murga punishment), for any mistake.This too was a reason why others were not okay with Nag's late night entries as the consequences of his follies would have been for everyone.

One Sunday morning Mr. Mand surprised everyone as he raided the hostel. Sunday mornings were exempted from morning drills so students would sleep till late. Mr. Mand straightway entered Nagroom to awake him.

"What is this?" Mr. Mand enquired pointing his swagger stick towards a carton box placed above his trunk box.

"Good morning sir." Nag was quick to wake up and stand on his bed. He wanted to jump down but there was no space.

"This is Visual Display Unit, to be submitted to science teacher, sir." Nag answered with utmost sincerity.

Mr. Mand fell for the wit and alacrity shown by Nag and feeling convinced, quickly left the room; the Nagroom. Mr. Mand thought it was some science project and therefore ignored. Mr. Mand had only heard of VDU and VCR and never bothered to know about the full forms.

Nag had brought a VCR/VDU to launch the first show in P-2. He could have been in trouble had he not devised the technique of telling full form of the acronym.

CHAPTER THREE

FIRST DAY FIRST SHOW

Nag dispelled the situation highly diplomatically but an outside chance of getting caught still loomed. Should Mr. Mand cross-verify it from science teacher there was every chance of being caught. Nag was still desperate to watch the movie. He waited till Mr. Mand left for a shopping spree to nearby Mandi town in the official Mahindra Jeep of the school. The Mahindra jeep pulling a small trolley two-chained with it would routinely go to the town to shop the food items for mess, and would invariably take wardens turn-wise.

Nag immediately called upon a small meeting of P-2 residents and revealed his plans about a movie show. There were some initial hiccups but everyone fell for the persuasion and excitement. The matter got more than settled when first benchers also agreed to join.

The room adjoining Nagroom was selected for the screening. Normally there were no curtains so idea of covering windows with bed sheets was dropped, so that no passerby could doubt anything fishy. The television set was put on lower berth of the bed on window side, to rule out the possibility of screen being spotted from outside. Moreover the room had its window towards the backyard which was not a thoroughfare unless someone was there on purpose. The gate at the main entrance was bolted from inside. The timings were set in such a way that movie would finish well before lunch so that no one could doubt as lunch time was one such occasion when movement was more frequent outside.

It was the first big misdoing on our part so there were apprehensions. A very small noise or footfall outside would make us to shut down the VDU, and we would do that only to discover that there was none. After couple of occasions we stopped and restarted the screening, VCR developed some problem and it didn't play the cassette.

No one of us including Nag had any idea how to fix the problem. We were just waiting anxiously.

"Let me see." Neeraj jumped from upper berth to have a look.

"Do you know how it works?" Asked Nag.

"I know", said Neeraj while having a look at the system.

He carefully took the cassette out, cleaned it softly using his clean white hanky. He unscrewed two front screws and opened the upper plate.

"Its head needs to be cleaned. Oh! its belts also need to be cleaned. Can someone give me brand new one rupee note?" Neeraj enquired after spotting the fault.

Pankaj was the most decorated student who would keep things nice and tidy in his trunk box. Everyone turned to him.

"I have some new currency notes but I am not sure about one rupee note." Pankaj said while jumping immediately to open his trunk box.

Thankfully Pankaj discovered many one rupee notes in his trunk box. Neeraj cleaned the head and belts carefully and VCR resumed functioning. The movie ended well in time.We had our lunch, but then came the biggest task.

The VCR and the Television set was hired by seniors residing in other hostel, which Nag had brought to P-2 on the condition that he would return it before 2 PM so as to avoid extra charges. He needed someone to escort him and his search zeroed in on me. I was reluctant initially but fell shortly to Nag's persuasions.

We wrapped both VCR and television set in different cartons and lifted one-each on our shoulders. We gatecrashed from the backyards and speeded in no time towards a place called Teen-Peepal, which was around one and half kilometers away from our school. We reached safely without being noticed, deposited the Visual Display system and turned back.

We had hardly walked two minutes when our school jeep stopped just a few meters past us. We took notice of it and also of Mr. Sawan Singh Mand who was sitting adjacent to driver. Nag in no time insinuated to turning right and keep walking without panicking till we covered a fair bit of distance. Just after two minutes we took the short cut to miss the main road and in ten minutes we were back in hostel.

Mr. Sawan Singh Mand on reaching hostel summoned everyone out. He was surprised that P-1, P-3, and P-4 were busy playing inter kothi cricket matches in ground while entire P-2 students were in hostel itself.

"Amit Nag, you come out. Who was other man with you? Ask him to come out as well." Sawan Singh Mand ordered sounding furious.

Nag came out calmly and stood beside Mr. Mand.

"I told you to ask other man to come out and stand with you as well." Mand reiterated.

"I was all alone sir. I needed to buy a geometry box but couldn't get it. I had gone to your room for permission but it was locked sir." Nag explained politely.

A powerful slap on Nag's face disturbed the silence.

"Who was the other fellow with you? This is the last time I am asking." Mr. Mand threatened Nag clutching his cheeks.

"Believe me sir. There was no one with me." Unperturbed Nag stood his ground firmly.

"Shall I come out and reveal it's me". I was in a fix and in awe.

Nag in the process was trying to teach the prodigies the first lesson but wasn't sure how long the toddlers could hold.

Just when Nag noticed that Mand was not looking at him, he put his first figure on his lips and made every one of us to take a serious note of it.

"Come what may, we won't reveal anything." The words were never said but were best conveyed and understood.

Some of us were hardly ten, still crying for missing their parent, some of us would bathe to leave soap in ear, some of us couldn't even comb their hair, and some of us would start crying even if scolded, but what Nag had gestured silently was loud and clear to every P-2'ian that day.

"Okay, he doesn't know, someone amongst you must know it. Lean against this wall, upside down, till the name is out." Mr. Mand commanded and we obeyed.

It's extremely difficult to be in that situation. Your entire body weight rests on your hands. Your head starts feeling the pressure, back aches badly.

Half an hour and he changed the punishment to squatting (Murga making). He would hit with his pointed key ring, the moment he saw anyone lowering his ass to relax for a while.

"Lift your letter boxes", was the command generally used by Mr. Mand for the purpose.

The punishments were changed frequently and lasted for three hours but everyone remained tightlipped that day. Mr. Mand was deeply disappointed at this. He enjoyed the sadistic pleasure but was still far away from victory. He would have continued but atleast three students fainted. Some of the seniors took note of it and complained.

Principal came to know about the punishment. Mr. Mand was even reprimanded later, though not in our presence. He was no longer the warden now. He was even transferred after few days.

It was victory for us. We had for the first time felt a sense of unity, a sense of organization. We grew more brotherly. We were sharing everything, pleasures and pains. No one from P-2 cried for missing his parents after that day. We had found brothers, and not to mention, Nag was our eldest brother.

CHAPTER FOUR

ACROSS THE RIVER

Navodaya school at Pandoh was situated right at the left bank of river Beas. The river though held a great deal by a big dam at Pandoh, could turn furious at times as more waters would warrant opening of the flood-gates of the dam. Of late there had been several causalities in the vicinity. The instructions therefore were very clear to all the students, to not to venture in or around the river, whatever be the reason.

Himalayan rivers have a unique tendency to attract or allure people towards them. It is sometimes their sublime water, sometimes their mysterious sound, sometimes their uneven flow and sometimes the reasons inexplicable.

River Beas named after ancient sage Beas, who probably worshipped somewhere around its origin at Beas-Kund, flew in a very attractive fashion. Anyone with slightest of imagination could easily personify it and conclude symbolically. Madam Sunita Malhotra was taking an arrangement class in a ground outside the classroom the other day. It was a small ground which was meant for morning assembly. When she found it slightly difficult to control the class she made us to write something, something we felt at that moment, most possibly in the form of poetry.

Chaman one of sincerest students ended up writing a poem on the river Beas.

"aa jao devi tum pavak ban kar beh jao", it started thus.

"Come Godess, and flow past like breeze."

Chaman had even explained this that it was river Beas which motivated him to pen down these lines. He was clearly visualising the river as Goddess. His efforts were lauded at various levels and the poem was even read in the morning assembly the following morning.

However, for those who couldn't imagine like Chaman, it unfolded an idea to go and actually see the Goddess. Most of us were villagers who had their little stints in rivulets or nullahs or the khuds as they were popularly termed, and that made many of us to swim a little.

One fine Sunday, on Nag's call many of us dared to see the river Goddess without caring whether we knew how to swim or not.

Nag first of all approached Chaman but he denied the proposal upfront. Chaman was a strict disciplinarian and would seldom disobey diktats. Nag however was hell bent that day and he continued his expedition with the volunteers.

Reaching riverside, it was such a pleasure. The sands on its flood plains were warm enough to allow us to take our clothes off and role on, to play games, to write names on sand. However, the real fun was to take a dip which no one could spearhead.

It was Dhani Ram, the man most shy of us who jumped into the river and in no time crossed it to reach the other side. No one could believe this from Dhani Ram. He was a short boy who most of the times had looked diffident only. He was also not very happy because of his family circumstances. He would stammer a little and that prevented him from talking much.

Dhani Ram was an exceptional swimmer though, he proved that day. He jumped into the river and in no time emerged at the other side. There were many who knew the skill but it was never easy to jump into a river and especially when no one had ever swum beyond nullahs, khuds or very small rivulets. Dhani Ram signaled all of us to join him the other side. He looked very happy in his tailored underwear, with water oozing from just around everywhere his body. And as he giggled, there was clearly a sense of happiness or sense of liberation on the face of Dhani ram.

In a moment's time most of us were on the other side of the river. Those left didn't either know how to swim, or couldn't dare to negotiate the undercurrent of river. While most amongst the left outs were happy to stay back and enjoy vicariously, two of us were itching to go to the other side.

Amit Nag didn't know how to swim while I couldn't collect the guts. Both of us were standing on a big riverside rock which served as the high diving platform for the divers who ventured. Dhani Ram obviously realized the dilemma and swam back doing a jackknife to allure us further into the act.

Amit Nag admitted honestly that he didn't know how to swim. Even I ranted the same reason, may be because I didn't want to sound diffident. Though I knew I could swim but the river proved a deterrent.

Dhani Ram straightway started coaching and was soon joined by few others. After swimming with assistance for about half an hour Nag claimed that he has mastered the skill. I on the other hand wasn't sure about me.

Nag was the chosen first for crossing over amongst two of us. Men were properly deployed by Dhani Ram at strategic positions. Some were tasked with rescue operations even, if that be the case. Nag dived headfirst and emerged after some time; he did struggle but was safely received at the other end.

It was my turn then. I recalled my deities and dived headfirst. I hadn't done that before (the diving), and kind of lost myself beneath for a while. Though I emerged without any effort of mine, but in the process lost my endeavor to move my hands and feet, the necessary pre requisite to swim. As a result water kept me dragging with its flow downstream. Realizing I have been dragged a fair bit, I lost the application of mind and kind of surrendered to the flow. The water which apparently appeared still had powerful undercurrent. Though I managed to keep my head out for a breather but I wasn't actually swimming, and was always moving away from rest of my fellows.

"Swim, move your hands and feet", were the shouts I overheard but I was always moving away.

The rescue team jumped in but they couldn't get hold of me. Dhani Ram was closest to get to me but he was short, thin and weak and couldn't help me.

Nag jumped into the fray though he himself had struggled to reach the other end and was of course a debutant himself. He swam confidently to reach me. He was a powerful man so he pulled me over him and continued swimming sidereal downstream. Within no time we hit the bank and that ended my rescue. As we were walking back, I was still in awe while all my fellows were laughing loudly. Chaman's poem, was still reverberating in my mind, "aa jao devi tum pavak ban kar bah jao".

CHAPTER FIVE

MANDAL COMMISION & THE FIRE

A year later we successfully moved into class seven,though nothing important resulted to be highlighted. All higher academic ranks were clinched by other students, mostly the girls. Nag managed to pass the exams comfortably but couldn't find a place in Sandhu sir's dream team. Though he was always in the dugout but Sandhu Sir never played him. He was however promised a berth in the next year's squad. May be Sandhu sir wanted the prodigy to mature a bit more before he could actually hit the turf.

It was in the year 1990, the August, when V.P. Singh Govt. declared its intent to implement the report of Mandal Commission, leading to widespread student protests all across the country. Mandal Commission or the Socially and Educationally Backward classes Commission (SEBC) was established in India by Janta Party Govt. under Prime Minister Morarji Desai with a mandate to identify the socially and educationally backward classes of India. The

Commission had recommended that members of Other Backward Classes (OBC's) be granted reservations to 27% of jobs under Central Govt. and Public Service Undertakings.Though the report was submitted in the year 1980 but Govt. decided to implement it ten years later.

The school premises was a closed system having no connect with outside world. We the students inside didn't even understand the politics and the caste dynamics of India. It was only one other day when a mob of 50 to 100 agitators stormed our campus and forced the classes to get over. Our Principal and teachers were manhandled while they were trying to control the rampaging mob.

"All institutes are closed. There won't be any class from now on, or we will set the classrooms ablaze", warned the leader of the mob. Most of the persons in the crowd were identifiable as they used to come to our school ground to play basketball. Our ground though demarcated to be a school property, was still used by outsiders for want of a boundary wall. Sometimes there were matches played, and sometimes even minor scuffles would take place between outsiders and Sandhu Sir during our games period. The scuffles would sometimes warrant the involvement of our seniors as well. The senior most class was class 10 then, so there was good number of volunteers who were ready to rub their shoulders even with comparatively older students from outside. Some of the outsiders occasioned this unrest/protest as an opportunity to settle their scores. Even from agitation's point of view they hadn't entered the campus with clean hands. Some of them had the girls of our school in mind, while the others had the lady teachers on their radar. The protest across the country was largely of students but the crowd which had entered our campus was constituted by even vegetable and fruit sellers of Pandoh market. The person who hired VCR to students was also seen in the crowd. Many of them wanted to have a glimpse of campus which was normally out of bounds for them.

This sudden intrusion was successfully repelled by authorities with Sandhu Sir at the forefront. It soon subsided. There was an agreement though, "The school authorities would not allow the classes to go in any case." The crowd understood that this was a residential school and a complete shutdown like other state schools was not perhaps possible.

The school authorities immediately had a meeting thereafter and came out with an alternative plan. "The classes would go in two sessions, one during the morning drills till 8 o' clock and the other during the preparatory classes in the evening before dinner."

This arrangement worked well as no one from outside could notice it. The students were relaxed with the compulsion of uniforms. Besides, all other routines like morning assembly were put under suspension for a while. During the daytime students would stay at hostel and would do homework or play around.

The arrangement worked well for about a week till the crowd barged one more time into the campus. This time it was more rampaging and went on to break the tube lights in some of our classrooms. They left with some stringent warnings this occasion. The crowd this occasion was somewhat more serious and there seemed a cause to their agitation. It comprised largely of students rather than like the previous one which had hawkers in it.

"How would they know but?" This was the question doing rounds in the discussions of campus. It was concluded emphatically that someone amongst us must have informed them. The teachers were still guessing while the name was already doing rounds amongst the students.

The school authorities met again in an emergency meeting and assessed losses. The event necessitated an evacuation plan as student's security, including that of girls, couldn't have been compromised. The plan was unfolded to our delight. The students who could message their parents to come to school could go home. This resulted in perhaps the biggest information dissemination within a couple of days as the campus turned almost empty. This became possible because once a student was taken home he/she informed everyone in the vicinity. There were no bus services so parents used either scooters or shared cabs on hiring and many a time the students of entire locality were taken in batches. School authorities allowed this on written undertakings from parents who couldn't have come themselves but authorized others to take their wards. Some senior students even managed local guardians to secure leave and left on their own thereafter. Authorities were also not very strict as there was already a message from the Head Quarters to decongest the campuses as far as possible. Only those students would stay whose houses were either far way or in high risk zone, or whose parents couldn't somehow come to receive their wards. Many teachers also proceeded on leave, leaving the campus a desolated place with merely 40 odd students and around 10 teachers including Sandhu sir.

Amongst the students left, majority were from junior classes, including me and Nag. Nag was upset as he desperately wanted to go home but his brother in law didn't show up. He was in the process of arranging a local guardian even, but it failed as the person he arranged was renowned for his notoriety and was recognized by the warden. My parents on the other hand were never too eager to take me home and besides I didn't have neighbors in the school. Land line telephones were still a sparsely availed luxury.

We somehow come to terms with the situation prevalent and started enjoying it gradually. Lesser number of students automatically meant an improvement in quality of food, more access on sporting gears, and above all, more leisure time. The situation outside in the meanwhile had worsened. Three video coach buses were torched just outside the campus of our school. The news of self-immolation of a student in the nearby Mandi town had reached the campus. The situation had turned so tense that even if our parents wanted to come they couldn't have made it. Public transport was called off and only private vehicles were plying, that too in emergency only.

Our school had a Mahindra jeep which would routinely go to Mandi town to collect essentials for mess even during the troubled times. A two wheeled trolley would often be two- chained whenever it intended procuring ration. This had to be done in any case as it formed the part of essential services. However some fringe elements outside didn't take it in good taste. They were plotting something and it one day resulted into a small group's gatecrashing into school campus. They initially entered on the pretext of ensuring if the classes were off but their intentions were soon made clear when they approached the garage and made an attempt to torch it.

Sandhu sir dared the group almost single handedly as he didn't allow them to enter the garage. He held the gate stretching his arms and held his ground tightly. There was no one in the group who could surpass this tough built Jatt who won't relent, come what may. This infuriated the crowd and they left to come again with larger numbers.

This was the makeup time for all of us with suddenly a sense of unity ushering in. Sandhu sir picked some 10 volunteers, mostly from senior classes including two of us, Nag and me. We altogether assisted the driver of the jeep by making a makeshift road to a place inside the thick bushy cannabis jungle around the hostels. Thereafter we were instructed by Sandhu sir to remove the wheel marks. We were asked to undo the road again by placing some big logs and some large boulders so as to make it appear least likely for a jeep to move. Principal Sir in the meanwhile had called police but since it were deployed in areas more troubled and at distance, so we knew the cops won't make it too early.

The crowd reappeared again, this occasion a larger one, with more force and alacrity. They barged into the campus despite Sandhu sir's stiff resistance. They pushed us aside, the volunteers, the teachers, the driver, whoever came their way. However they couldn't find the vehicle in the garage. They ransacked the entire area where the Jeep could possibly be parked, but to no avail. Just to satisfy them they pelted the glasses of solar geysers to break them into pieces. Police arrived in the meanwhile. Crowd started dispersing but rather reluctantly. The effort was lauded so much so that we had our dinner together with all our teachers, mess cooks and the supporting staff. We were all congratulated for we had saved our jeep. We developed a very strong bond for rest of our stay during the troubled times.

CHAPTER SIX

THE THIRD LANGUAGE

The inception of our kind of school necessarily had to have an inherent ideology, and that ideology broadly translated into – national integration. One of the outcomes of principles of national integration was the migration system. The students from one school were picked to be migrated to some other school of some other state and vice-versa. In our case the school chosen was Karaikal in Tamil Nadu. Up to this it was all good but there was one more feature that was unpleasant about it; Tamil was introduced as a third language in our regular curriculum. Students found it the most difficult of the subjects they were taught, and there were very few who could master this southern language with a typically difficult script and pronunciation.

Mr. Ramanathan was vested with the duty of teaching this language to all Hindi speaking students who were least interested in. To add to the woes of Mr. Ramanathan, he didn't understand a word of Hindi himself. He however was a jovial fellow who often allowed his class to turn into a fun class. Students would mock him, call names in their native language, would gossip around and so on. Some others would complete the assignments of other subjects. Still there were few who would learn the Tamil poems by heart, would try to compound alphabets into words, words into and phrases and sentences. It were only those few in the class that Mr. Ramanathan would teach and rest were simply not paid much heed to.

Nag surprisingly had never failed in Tamil, despite the fact that he couldn't even write a word of it. This, which others would envy of Nag was a secret. He had never shared this secret with anyone. The monthly unit tests were on and everyone turned to Nag for some help and to decode for them the mantra. Nag had simple formula; he would copy. Copying or cheating in our school was not very common a practice so most of us didn't understand the petty nuances involved. Nag was straight forward in his lessons that it needed caution and depended on multiple factors including – who the invigilator was.

On the appointed day all who treated the language to be alien were carrying lot of small chits with them, with the answers to the probable questions, some of which were supposed to be exchanged midway. The luck had it that it was Mr. Sandhu who was assigned the duty in our class that day. The very first thing which Mr. Sandhu did was he changed the sitting arrangement.

As the exam progressed the students ventured to take on the eyes of Sandhu sir. Sandhu sir was prompt; within no time he confiscated every unfair mean to put it in dustbin. He even frisked students and offered them a chance to volunteer handing over everything they were carrying.

He added while cautioning – "if someone caught after this, take it guaranteed he/she is going to pack his/her bags – back home".

Students realized that it wasn't a fair idea to take on chances with Mr. Sandhu and the dustbin filled in no time. The exam resumed with an uneasy calm prevailing around.

Nag hadn't however surrendered anything and all eyes were on him, pondering, for how long he could escape the eyes of Sandhu sir. We all knew that Nag was carrying a lot of material with him, which Mr. Sandhu would catch sooner or later. It was just a matter of time.

Students had nothing to write on their answer sheets so they were just waiting for the time. Nag, who was sitting with a girl student didn't surrender anything but he couldn't use it either. This made him to reconsider his options. The girl besides being studious was also a very good sports person and was quite familiar with Nag. On occasions he had helped her scoring the basketball goal. They hadn't learnt the game well yet, but sportsman spirit had already started culminating.

She realized Nag was not able to write anything, neither was there any possibility of using anything from his hidden resources. She had completed her exam so had plenty of time to notice the movement of Mr. Sandhu who had to keep vigil on three rows, to and fro. She would expose her answers to him at right moments and he simply copied from her sheet, and ended up writing minimum answers required to be attempted. Everything was conveyed so succinctly with minimum of fuss, without being said anything. This is typical of sportspersons – they understand the team work.

Amongst the students fearing the subject, it was only Nag who managed to pass. Mr. Ramanathan had specially arranged for Mr. Sandhu's duty that day in our class and he was happy with the result that almost all failed, but Nag's success story was still a riddle to him.

It was just a few days later that we got the news that Mr. Ramanathan has been transferred and he will soon be replaced by a new teacher.

His replacement, Mr. Alexander was a very short man but extremely versatile. He has quickly come to terms with different climatic conditions of northern India. Within no time he has added in his vocabulary the customary phrases of Hindi. He could sing really well. He had himself composed a song, which was doing rounds in the campus. Even the students like us who understood nothing of Tamil were humming the song. All this while but, he hadn't been able to teach us even a single day. This was primarily due to the reason that he hadn't yet settled properly. He would often travel to Mandi for procuring coconut oil and other essentials. Sometimes Principal would call him to discuss his roles and assignments, and kept him away from our class for a good many number of days.

Finally the day arrived when Mr. Alexander walked into our classroom. We were all very excited as we wanted him to sing his trademark song for us. He first insisted on introduction however, and the students started introducing themselves in seriatim.

As the round of introduction progressed, in came Nag's turn. Nag was a tall boy and Mr. Alexander barely reached his shoulder. Nag introduced himself and Mr. Alexander couldn't gather what he said. Nag had very husky voice and his pronunciation wasn't also very clear. It had happened many a time in the past that he couldn't convey what he meant. This occasion he was communicating with a south Indian who had just joined and was still not very familiar with the typical north Indian names, so it was bound to happen.

Mr. Alexander was a very short fellow and therefore what Nag was saying was being transmitted overhead. A couple of attempts went in vain till Nag inadvertently held Mr. Alexander by his head and uttered his name loudly in one of the ears of Mr. Alexander. This somehow was not taken in a very good taste by Mr. Alexander.

"Hey! I am not deaf." Shouted Mr. Alexander as the whole class started laughing.

Nag on this recited some of the lines from the song of Mr. Alexander and patted on his back acknowledging that he was a great singer. This further infuriated Mr. Alexander and he in a rush shook Nag's hand off his back and tried to slap him on the face. Nag was tall so he managed to escape. The class was in a thrill but Mr. Alexander took at his heart. He desperately wanted to slap Nag. Nag started kidding him and in the process of all this Nag threw him apart which landed Mr. Alexander on a desk placed opposite to Nag's. Mr. Alexander injured himself badly. He woke up immediately and rushed to Principal's room.

Hell let lose for Nag just in a flash. The matter was immediately ordered to be enquired by a disciplinary committee constituted for the purpose. Nag surely made fun of his height but he never intended to cause any injury to Mr. Alexander. Committee recorded the statement of almost every student of the class but none could explain his innocence. Committee recommended action in very strong words. Because Nag was an athlete, Mr. Sandhu came to his rescue but that too didn't help. Next step would follow—and that was summoning of parents.

Nag had none of his parents surviving and that – kind of came to his rescue. It raised sympathy and a lenient view was expected. Both, his sister and brother-in-law were extremely apologetic. His brother-in-law thrashed him in everybody's presence. Things pacified after a seasoned senior teacher intervened. He spoke of counseling for the first time – and Nag was let off with a stern warning. His guardians had to write a written undertaking.

The episode had a severe effect on Nag's psyche and his behavior changed dramatically. He started picking up fights on minor issues and turned stubborn. No one from teaching faculty counseled him though. It were only us, his friends in his close circle who stood by him, talked to him and pacified him when occasioned.

CHAPTER SEVEN

THE SCUFFLE

The episode with Tamil teacher and the aftermaths had a deep impact on Nag's psyche. He was readily irritable and would often pick fights. He missed the annual sports meet which was hosted by a school other than ours this occasion. The contingent was to be as short as possible and that retrenched the athletes from junior classes to a great deal. This too led to frustration for Nag as he was consistently being part of those stiff morning drills in the hope of getting into that illustrious group of athletes who would represent their school in the annual sports meet. Nag had already thrashed at least two boys from the immediate senior class. He was already renowned as a tough nut to crack. Some would call him very gutsy and some would term him unbeatable.

The annual exams of class seven were announced. The session ended with the announcement of result with many of us including Nag, failing in Tamil. We were asked to reappear in supplementary exams. Nevertheless, students of class VIII as we were promoted into felt established in the school. Class VIII was a fairly senior class and we were enjoying it.

The senior most batch of our school had jumped to class XI. This was the batch we all would look up to; the students of class XI were the most sought after ones for any reason. Some of them had returned from Tamil Nadu after completing their two years of migration period. Students who returned from Tamil Nadu were fluent in English, and they would often boast about it. Most of them had grown whiskers and would therefore shave their faces. Their voices had turned husky. Some of them had excelled in swinging the cricket ball both ways. The others could score at will, while in the basketball field. The girls had grown up to be adored for their beauty and sensualities. They were chosen prefects of our cultural houses. They were not only consulted by teachers in the house meetings but their decisions mattered in those meetings. We would all look forward to them for whatever they did.

Nag himself was also ensnared by the skills of some of his seniors from class XI. He was particularly impressed with Harsha. Harsha hadn't been to Tamil Nadu though, but there was something about him which surfaced all of a sudden. With mediocre height Harsha was clean and tidy and would often dress well. He was a slim man but extremely agile. He was basically a Punjabi but his father served in BBMB, Bhakra Beas management Board, and they had settled permanently in Pandoh itself.

The primary reason for Nag's liking him was that Harsha could dance very well. His choice of songs appealed Nag a great deal. It so happened on occasions that Nag asked for his audio cassettes having Michael Jackson's songs which Harsha happily gave.

The other thing which Nag liked about Harsha was that he could swing the cricket ball. There were pacers in the school cricket squad but no one could swing the ball like

Harsha did. Nag could bat a good deal but had absolutely no defense to an in-swinging delivery from Harsha the other day when a friendly match was going on. It edged past to the keeper. Nag didn't even move, nor did his bat.

"Bhai how to ball that delivery, the one that you got me caught behind with"? Nag asked Harsha after the game was over.

"It's difficult to explain. I know it swings, but I don't know how. It's basically how you grip the ball. The stitches have to be in between your middle and index fingers with thumb holding the ball, and shinier side facing the batsman if you want to in-swing the ball (for a right handed bowler, Harsha was a right hander), and other way round if you want to out-swing the ball. This is in case of a relatively older ball. The new ball which shines equally on both sides will swing naturally, but then you have to angle it and pitch it at right place."

Harsha explained but he wasn't very sure he did it right, and he admitted to the fact that he doesn't fully understand the science of swing.

The explanation proved a little too technical for Nag as he couldn't understand the applied physics. Nag gathered that Harsha was arrogant and didn't want him to learn the skill.

It was morning assembly the other day. Mr. Sandhu was commanding from the stage.

"Attention,....... Stand at ease."

There was something yet to settle in last rows as students had to rush from different directions before assembling in the ground meant for the purpose. It was in this process of lining up that nag inadvertently pushed Harsha. Harsha a skinny boy just managed to hold himself as he could have fallen down. Harsha in all spontaneity abused Nag dragging his mother in. This was intolerable for Nag as he had lost his mother long back and he fondly loved her. Nag quickly got hold of Harsha's collar and could have thrashed him, but withdrew immediately as Sandhu sir shouted hard from the stage.

"I'll definitely hit him. He won't be spared". Nag whispered behind my back.

In the classroom I tried to pacify Nag but he won't yield. The clash looked imminent as seniors had taken note of it.

It was lunch time. All classes had queued up for lunch just outside the dining hall, with plates in their hands. Harsha along with a group was standing as a breakaway faction of the queue.

"What you were saying during the morning assembly, you........" Harsha shouted ferociously pointing towards Nag who hadn't noticed him till then.

Nag yelled on this and in no time pounced on him. It was just then when one other boy Hitesh attacked Nag. He held his neck in his arm and put him down. Hitesh launched the onslaught landing punches on Nag's face. Nag hadn't expected this. Hitesh was a very strong man who proved a little too much for Nag. The other seniors circled the scene as standbys, in case any of us dare intervening.

Every one of them was of firm belief that juniors mustn't cross their limits.

"Nag mustn't only pay for this daredevilry but the punishment should serve a deterrent."

There were some whispers in the crowd that even girls of class XI wanted Nag to be taught a lesson. There was a proper meeting in the class before the plan was actually executed.

Hitesh was helped by some of his mates as he withdrew. He dusted his pants, adjusted his disheveled coat and spared a glance on all of us.

"Class VIII, you all remain in your skins", announced Hitesh as he left for the mess with his entire team.

Nag had troubles rising up before he was helped. Once on his feet he shouted loudly before throwing his plate like a discus throw.

"You mother........,".

This was clearly heard by all the seniors. They were slightly taken aback with Nag's resurrection. It sure would have sent shivers to some of the faint-hearted seniors even. After all everyone was not Hitesh in class XI.

The message was loud and clear though. Nag was down but not defeated. Class XI was criticized unequivocally by every junior class and Nag was lauded for his stance.

Nag started crying after that. He straightway rushed to the hostel and refused to eat.

CHAPTER EIGHT

HOLI & THE AFTERMATHS

It was a delayed Holi this year; in the month of April. The festival though celebrated by all had some special fervor for some in our school. Most of our teachers were from Punjab and Haryana and that made them all the Holi enthusiasts. Sandhu Sir obviously stood at the forefront of things. Any such occasion and we would be rallied to a big ground some distance away. It was called helipad, though helicopter seldom landed on this bumpy surface with untrimmed grass all around.

We all gathered around morning assembly ground on a call. We were distributed colures in small packets before we were instructed to march in threes on the left side of road, the National Highway no. 21. For lunch puri-sabzi was in the menu, to be cooked and served on the helipad itself. Our mess cooks had already left with all their paraphernalia in our school jeep.

National Highway (NH-21) was a two-lane road connecting Delhi and Leh. Traffic was not too heavy but still the road was busy. It had Manali on its way, a place frequented by tourists. The big and large convoys of army would keep the road busy once Rohatang Pass was thrown open in summers. HRTC buses were less frequent and timely but lot of private vehicles would keep speeding their ways.

One other feature of this road was that it served as time saver for drivers. It was mostly leveled and was perfectly metalled. The drivers would often speed their vehicles to cover up the time lost in negotiating curvy ascents and descents before and after that plain patch of some 50 kilometers between Sundernagar and Pandoh. Otherwise also the road alongside river Beas would often invite drivers to put the pedal on accelerator.

Such being the scenario it wasn't wise to take the entire school to a faraway place and that too on Holi. Some of the senior teachers opined thus and refused to be a party to it. However Sandhu sir had had it with Principal and many young teachers backed him. We all took to the road, marching, singing and dancing. Colors were being thrown into one another and the mob soon gathered momentum to turn into a massive Holi procession.

As the crowd traversed certain distance it even took to blocking the passage of vehicles, forcing the commuters to offer their cheeks for colors to be applied on. Some speeding vehicles would start speeding further on the sight of crowd blocking them and then stopping suddenly just in front. It was all exciting but extremely risky. Still with Sandu sir leading from the front did help arresting many fears.

Mr. Ashok was a young school clerk who was patrolling to and fro on his Bajaj Chetak scooter with someone else riding pillion. It so happened that the leading group in the crowd started blocking Ashok sir's scooter also. Ashok sir would stop just a few yards behind, take about turn and would speed away to come back again after a while. This turned out to be new adventure and the crowd stopped intercepting other vehicles. They instead focused all their energies on Bajaj Chetak scooter which played hide and seek.

Sensing this bizarre euphoria everyone who possibly could, became part of the leading group. Nag and his close mates in no time broke apart from their parent group and joined the first line of defense.

Ashok sir this occasion appeared with relatively higher speed, as if he intended to break deep into the crowd.

Eyeing this Sandhu sir exclaimed! "We mustn't allow him to pierce into. Stand firmly on your ground."

Ashok sir on the other hand believed firmly that reckoning the speed crowd would make way for him. He raced but realized that crowd won't relent. He applied brakes but that was little too late and scooter rammed into Amit Nag while Ashok Sir tried to take turn to avoid clash. The scooter fell along with riders but it was only Nag who picked injury around his hip bones, the ilium in particular.

It soon ended the frenzy. Ashok sir immediately picked Nag and drove him to hospital. The BBMB hospital at Pandoh referred him to zonal hospital Mandi as we soon saw Ashok sir driving back towards Mandi. He didn't reveal much but stopped for a while to discuss something with Sandhu sir only and sped away in no time. Nag was sitting in between the Ashok sir and the other man who was riding pillion. Nag looked in pain but no one could manage to know the exact extent of his injury.

We were all told to not to report the incident to Principal and to other senior teachers who weren't part of the crowd. The celebration turned a low key affair with just lunch at helipad and getting back quietly, walking sideways avoiding even the charcoal clad road.

Sympathy aroused for Nag amongst all irrespective of classes. Even Hitesh and Harsha were waiting for the updates. The girls in particular were very sad, including the ones who had approved his public thrashing the other day.

We reached hostel and so did the update about Nag. X-Ray confirmed that the bone was intact and the wound which required dressing was only an outer injury. It would require some time to heal and Nag was advised rest.

Ashok sir arranged for his medicines and all, and would confirm his wellbeing every day. Nag was convalescing well but he had to avoid bathing. This resulted in some typical kind of itching and allergies around his pubic areas. The wound healed but his skin disease worsened. He won't show it to the compounder out of hesitation. It worsened further and engulfed the entire area resulting in genital rashes and spread of bumps.

This time around Sandhu sir would start special training sessions for sports persons. He summoned all sports persons during the games period confirming that Annual Sports Meet was announced to take place in our school by the authorities. As he took roll call from the list he had, he found Nag to be missing.

"What happened Amit, why aren't you too excited about it this occasion?" Sandhu sir asked Nag while he appeared tottering.

"I'm not well sir; I won't be able to play"

"What troubles you? You tell me. I'll get it fine. There is still some time to go."

Nag didn't tell anything though he was persuaded till last. Everyone thought he hadn't recovered from that injury.

Parents would visit the school on first Sunday of every month, though it wasn't a very strictly followed routine. Nag's sister and brother in law came to see him after a very long time. On seeing his condition his sister straightway applied for leave which was granted. This however meant that he won't make it to the drills and would miss the sports meet this occasion as well.

Sports meet was a very big event. All sportsperson clad in white jerseys and white shorts were hanging around just before the final rehearsal of the march past. Teams were to start reaching from the evening itself. Two days to go and Sandhu sir wanted to have that rehearsal in actual outfit.

"After this the uniforms would go to washing and there won't be more rehearsals. The opposition(s) mustn't have even an idea of what we are all for." Sandhu sir commanded.

Nag appeared all of a sudden with all energy and freshness. He wanted Sandhu sir to notice him and showed up but the teams were already done. Sandhu sir merely enquired about his health and moved on.

School did exceptionally well that year. All the gold medals, all the shields, all the team events, Navodaya Vidyalaya Pandoh stood right at the top. Class VIII yielded new heroes who did exceedingly well. Crowd was cheering the newly arrived stars. Nag was watching all this from the crowd. He was a forgotten hero now.

CHAPTER NINE

THE TRAGEDY

One of the biggest challenges the school had to face was to cater to the medical care of the students. It had one post of a pharmacist sanctioned which after Sawan Singh Mand's transfer remained vacant for some time. For some time it was occupied by a lady sister and after she managed her transfer it went to one Mr. Bhatt who was a Kashmiri Pandit. Mr. Bhatt was a jolly person whose medical acumen was seriously doubted by students. To save him from the disgrace he was to function from a very small dispensary having very limited supply of drugs. The school dispensary in the name of medical equipments had only one thermometer, some bandages and a weighing machine. The drugs in Bhatt's kit include only some antipyretics and some analgesics. There was a very strong, stinky ointment for skin diseases which students with skin rashes won't often apply. However Bhatt's popular treatment was his refusal to even entertain students complaining medical problems. Paani shani piyo theek ho jaoge (have some water and you will be alright).

This clichéd prescription of Bhatt would either ameliorate students or they won't fall sick at all. Whatever the reasons, it worked for majority of the students. Besides it served as a deterrent for those who would fake aches in order to miss the morning drills of Sandhu Sir or to miss some other important assignment.

No one really had any idea what happened to Amar, who was a student of class X. He probably had pneumonia which Mr. Bhatt tried to treat with his limited knowledge and resources but Amar didn't wake up next morning. He departed without showing too many symptoms. Resultantly Mr. Bhatt was soon at the receiving end. The news unfolded all of a sudden and left everyone more than just shocked.

Amar was one of those students who won't talk too much and would enjoy his own limited circle. He was from a not a well to do family. His parents were called and body handed over in a rush. This infuriated the senior classes and they gradually started grouping around.

Madhurendra, a class XI student took the lead. Lot many students rallied around him. He addressed the small grouping.

"This is a complete failure of school administration. With zonal hospital only 17 kilometers away, what prevented authorities from taking Amar to hospital. This smacks of some inaction, antipathy and even conspiracy. No FIR was registered, no postmortem done. The authorities want to save Bhatt. We will not sit silent. We demand justice for our brother."

"We want justice....we want justice". The sloganeering followed.

Madhurendra, one of brilliant students, wasn't just into the academics. He was a very good athlete, a quiz master. He was tall man with fair complexion; his hair would toss while he ran. He hadn't grown whiskers and that made his face look glossy. He was rebellious no doubt but that had attracted him towards misdoings even. He therefore was an irritant to many teachers despite being exceptional on many fronts.

The school administration swung into action. All the junior classes were instructed to keep away from the protesting site. They were rather made to sit in the classes. Teachers hurriedly gave some assignments. Everyone around remained tightlipped.

Madhurendra garnered enough support by then and two senior most classes, class X, and class XI were already sitting at a protest site and demanding a magisterial enquiry into all this. Principal's every effort and assurance failed to convince the agitating students.

We had no idea what we could do but Amit Nag was boiling within. He stood all of sudden and vociferously asked "What the hell we are doing here?"

"I think we must join the people sitting around school gate." Nag clarified his intentions.

It was not however easy to convince the students of class VIII to rise in rebellion against their teachers.

The biggest concern of authorities was that the students were sitting beside the main gate, exposing the incident to outside world. Principal fielded his best diplomats amongst the teachers, Mr. Sandhu, Principal sir's wife herself, and then eventually Principal himself with folded hands, but students won't relent.

The news travelled. Some journalists were spotted outside the gate and Madhurendra already talking to them. By evening some of us in the class VIII were agitated enough to join the protest. With blankets in our hands we all moved ignoring the warden who was tasked to stop us. Nag took the lead and we all followed. It was very cold at the protesting site but emotions ran high to beat the cold.

We had all refused to eat our dinner and this added to the problems of school authorities. The news reached us that Amar was cremated. Madhurendra was adamant on the intervention of District administration.

At 10'o clock in the evening SDM arrived but imposed a condition that we must shift to classroom before he could talk. A seasoned administrator readily acceded to the demand of a fair inquiry and made sure we had our dinner before going to sleep in our hostels. It was fair deal and students felt relieved.

Bhatt was missing from the site though. He was strategically taken to some unknown location within the school premises. Some students even connived to thrash him but he wouldn't show up. The pressure was however mounting on him. Students, particularly the senior ones boycotted the classes on second consecutive day and kept patrolling the quarters of Bhatt. They had some minor altercations and scuffles with teachers even.

At 4'o clock Bhatt showed up but he collapsed on the road just outside the administrative block. He had consumed something poisonous. Some said it was some kind of acid but no one was sure. Students rushed to help but they were warned to not to touch him by one of the senior teachers. He was immediately taken to hospital in our school jeep.

The incident somehow shifted the goalposts. Bhatt's action was not enough to vindicate him but still, flames of anger against him certainly calmed down. The agitating students withdrew. Some lady teachers including some senior girl students started fainting. This resulted in mass hysteria. The school was in real trouble. Things only improved the next day when the news came in that Bhatt's life has been saved.

There was no FIR registered. The postmortem was already out of question as the body was cremated. The enquiry committee's report was never shared with students. Authorities were allowed to buy more time to allow things to settle. In the name of Amar a cricket trophy was announced to be played once in every year. Bhatt managed transfer after some time and business started as usual.

CHAPTER TEN

BLACK LIST

Tamil had continued to be the third language despite the fact that the migration venue had changed from Tamil Nadu to Meghalaya. We had already exchanged a batch of students with Jawahar Navaodaya Vidyalaya Baghmara, a quaint little village in South Garo Hills, barely some three kilometers away from Bangladesh border. Garo was the native spoken language, a dialect yet to be ascribed the status of a language and hence the spectre of Tamil as third language still loomed.

Migration followed in class IX and we were just one class away. Our seniors who had migrated to Meghalaya were all praise for the place. They had grown long hair and that was an indication enough that freedom and independence found utmost importance in the school they were migrated to. There were already some discussions as to who all would go next year. Nag and his coterie were already showing lot of interest.

The incident of our joining that infamous protest had invited the wrath of teachers.

Our class teacher would often taunt us, "you can't be asked to do anything, or else you will sit beside the gate with your blankets."

We were kind of struck in the campus of school and were desperately looking for avenues, for escaping routes.

There used to be a lot of pressure on Principal and teachers to come out with a very good result of CBSE Board classes which included class X and class XII. Therefore one of the criteria picked by authorities was that of migration of underperforming students to improve their own school's result. But this occasion they had some different yardsticks in mind.

The other day our class teacher announced it openly that she's been asked to prepare a black list of students who will be ousted to faraway north-east. Only one third of the total strength of students would go. In our case the number came down to 19. Even if joining the protest was a criterion, one still needed to compete, as fairly large number of students had participated in the protest. We were all therefore keeping our fingers crossed.

The seniors already migrated had shared some glorified details about the place we were looking forward to go to for further studies, for coming two years; class IX and X. The school hadn't enforced anything very strictly. It was a delight for non-vegetarians; fish, pork and mutton were served frequently. A dozen of bananas would cost only one rupee. You could always wear a hairstyle of your own choice. If you had even the minutest of interest in western music and hard rock, you would relish your stay there. Teachers never beat students, football almost a religion there, and above all, the girls were very friendly.

This was too much an invitation from the distant north east. In order to improve the rankings in that illustrious black list, Nag and the coterie were already exploring follies which could be termed crimes. We did everything possible, picking fights, bunking classes, missing morning drills, misbehaving with teachers and what not.

Though our parents had given an undertaking confirming to the migration policy of school right at the time of admissions, still we were given a form to give our willingness and that was later sent to our parents for their final approval.

All calculations were done. All permutation and combinations worked. By the end of the year we had a fair idea who would go and who would not. This was possible because we knew whose parents would sign the letter and whose won't. In the end it was very clear that all in Nag's coterie but Nag were probables. It was only Nag who was doubtful. This was because of Nag's brother-in-law, who wouldn't allow Nag to go at any cost.

Nag knew it better than anyone else did. He also knew that it won't happen automatically and would require efforts. He therefore connived with postman and asked him to handover the letter to him rather than to the school clerk. Postman obliged and Nag in no time converted the No into Yes and handovered the letter back to the post man, who then delievered it in routine. This all had to be done before exams. And came the exams and we studied very hard and left no stone unturned. Failing in exam could possibly have proven to be another deterrent realizing our dream of going to our dreamland. We made sure that even Tamil would see us through.

After the exams were over school closed for holidays and we left for our homes after the results were announced. Hard work had paid the dividends and all of us passed comfortably.

"The students to be migrated will be informed during the holidays, and they will come all prepared as they will depart straight to their new school soon after the school

reopens."
Thus read the notice board of school.
We all left with so many doubts in our minds.

MEGHALAYA BOUND

The students bound for Meghalaya came to know about it through a postal communication from the school. It was as expected. We all found our place in the illustrious list but the main protagonist--- Nag was missing. His non-inclusion did upset all of us but our own inclusion had made way for compensating the huge loss. It was all contemplated by Nag but unfortunately he himself wasn't there when it came to reaping the dividends.

We all reached school all prepared, with a hold-all backpack, imitating our seniors or the way we were advised by them. A backpack was easy to carry while shuttling between different railway stations, and the chances of its misplacing or theft were meager while in trains. It could easily have been converted into a sleeping bag or used as a cushion or as a pillow.

We were all congratulated by all and subsequently summoned by Mr. Sandhu who was to escort us along with a lady teacher. We lined up just outside the Principal office. Mr. Sandhu started taking a roll call but the counting fell one short. Initially he thought he made a mistake but results always yielded the same count till someone pointed out that Chaman was missing.

Chaman's name was there in the list but he never received the letter in this regard as sent by the school administration. He was busy preparing his bedding, arranging his books etc after the long break. He stopped doing so only after he received a message that Mr. Sandhu wanted to see him immediately.

Chaman was caught unaware. He had no idea he was going to Meghalaya. His parents had already bid bye to him after having dropped him in the school. He hadn't packed suitably to go to the distant Meghalaya, and moreover he couldn't have gone without his parent's knowledge.

Decision had to be taken quickly. Chaman denied going too far a distance without intimating his parents and for he was not even informed. A couple of meetings with Principal made it clear that there was no way Chaman could stay back. The list of students to be migrated was already communicated to the Regional Office Chandigarh, to Head Office Delhi, to Ministry of Human Resources and Development at Delhi, and to the school authorities at Meghalaya. The message was conveyed to Chaman.

Chaman had to relent but still he proposed that he wanted to see his parents before leaving to an arduous journey of five days. This request of Chaman was conceded to by autorities.

Chaman's place was not a very distant one but it was already 7 in the evening and the buses were out of question to a very small village near Dhumavati temple, some 8 kilometers from Mandi town making the total travel from Pandoh to some 25 kilometers. Chaman decided to take the shorter route by actually trekking the distance. Going via road one actually had to travel to Mandi first and then come back taking almost a U-turn to reach Dhumavati and then the Chaman's place called Kotmorse. This circumnavigation could have been avoided a great deal going straight but via a typical labyrinth and that too during night time.

Chaman was daring but reasonable; he decided to take the help of one of his relatives from Pandoh. The man he picked for the purpose was his Dunty Dadu, as he dearly called him. He was actually the brother of Chaman's grandmother.

70 years old Dunty Dadu would always walk with a stick in his hands. He was extremely agile at this age even. Dunty Dadu had already gone to sleep actually when Chaman woke him up to narrate the ordeal he was subjected to. Dunty Dadu readied in no time with his stick and a very dim torch whose battery was about to exhaust. The duo of experience and exuberance together started the journey involving two major mountainous ascents and a descent. Torch had to be used judiciously and hence was used only when they discovered that they were off track. It was a rainy season so there were intermittent showers as well.

After the testing two hours, the duo reached Dhumavati, the temple of Godess---Dhuan Devi. There was a lonely house there and Dunty Dadu's torch had already given up. The duo decided to take some help ignoring the barking dogs guarding the house. Dunty Dadu requested some dry shoots of Bihul (Grewia Optiva), the native tree so that they could be used to serve as torches after being lit. Chaman's house was still at distance and they couldn't have done without light amongst the treacherous labyrinths with the fear of wildlife looming large.

At around 2'o clock the duo reached home. Everyone in the house woke up to the unexpected news. Chaman's mother soon came to terms with it and allowed him and Dunty Dadu to sleep for some time and started packing for Chaman. Chaman's father was out and it was only his mother who had to take a call and the daring lady took it in no time.

At 4'o clock in the morning they started the journey other way around. They climbed down to Mandi this occasion, embarked a bus from Mandi town. At 5'o clock in the morning Chaman was back in the school when most of his fellows were still fast asleep.

CHAPTER TWELVE

THE ADIEU

On appointed day we woke up unusually early, without the bell tolling for morning drills. The school mess had arranged for early breakfast. We were discussing the itinerary. It was a five days long journey.

We were supposed to reach Joginder Nagar and board the toy train for Pathankot. From Pathankot we were to catch Lohit express for Guhawati, a 60 hours arduous journey traversing the entire northern expanse. From Guwahati it was an overnight journey to Tura and then another half a day bus journey to the place called Baghmara, the place we were bound for.

Plenty of excitement was doing rounds, sending shrills down our throat. Chaman's overnight adventure had already provided the initial thrust for the upcoming journey.

We were 19 students of class IX, 12 boys and 7 girls, who were accompanied by equal number of students from class X. Mr. Sandhu was to escort us and his newly wedded wife was also travelling with him. Besides, Ms. Umang was also to escort the group, considering the fact that there was fairly a large number of girls in the group. It was comparatively a huge contingent so it required good escorts.

Ms. Umang taught economics to senior classes but was very familiar with the students of almost every class. She would often walk into any class that was free and start deliberating, discussing and having fun. One of the most important things of her persona was that she had developed a special connection with students. She could recall us by our names which wasn't the case with many other teachers. This always smiling, bob cut lady would resemble a European, not just in complexion and the physical appearance but her accent was also Anglicized. This made the students to strike a chord with her and this probably was the reason she was picked for this important assignment alongside Mr. Sandhu.

We left well in time bidding bye to all. We reached Mandi to change the bus for Jogindernagar, a quaint old town which actually was a British find. The presence of railway line confirmed the antiquity of town. The Shanan Power Project must have necessitated the railway line –the narrow gauge.

We could have travelled straight to Pathankot in the bus itself and reached early but the train fairs were cheaper and school authorities wiser. Anyways it was first time we were to board train except for few, so we were happy in any case.

As we alighted in Joginder Nagar Bus-stand we were asked to assemble in a rain shelter and take a look if our entire luggage was with us, before we could proceed to railway station which was at a walking distance.

As we stood I saw two eyes consistently gazing us from behind the closed window of a roadways bus bound for Mandi. It was rainy season and we had witnessed a constant drizzle throughout our journey. It was still the same story till we reached Joginder Nagar; the rain hadn't stopped.

There was a slight haze due to fog and it wasn't easy to guess from the distance who it could be.

I realized in a moment that there was some movement of hands, someone trying to waive from inside the bus, behind the window. I couldn't help myself venturing into rain and find who it was. As soon as I reached beside the bus the window opened. Amit Nag was sitting along with his brother in law who was escorting him back to Pandoh.

Sighting Nag all others from our class rushed to see him. His brother in law didn't look too happy about it as rain drops were making their way into through the opened window, but neither Nag cared about him nor did we. We shook hands one last time. We didn't say anything, we couldn't say anything. Nag was visibly upset but continued to smile with his moist eyes. As the bus started rolling down the slope we all stood helpless with the posture akin to - stand at ease.